Maggie & Fever

A Sasquatch Story

By Christopher Noel

Maggie had a hairy friend
But no one quite believed her.
He lived just around the bend
And she had named him Fever.

Why this name? Because the morning
She first saw him, she was sick.
And Mama said, "Your face is burning,
Your eyes are playing tricks."

But after dark, she heard a little
Friendly finger-tapping sound.
Then sunup showed her, on the sill,
A stone all smooth and round.

Now Maggie knew without a doubt
That Fever was the truth.
And after this, she ventured out
Along the bending path.

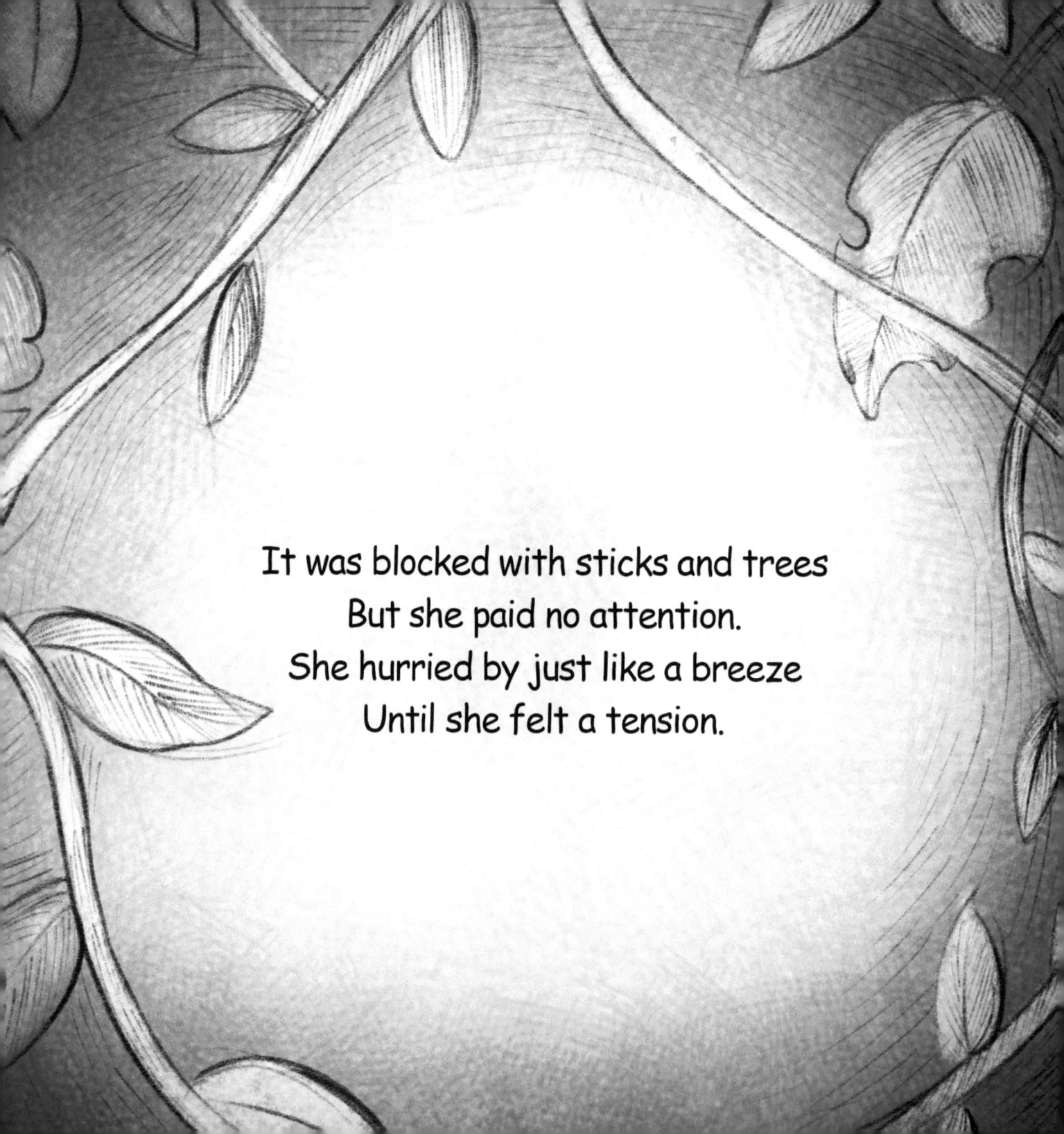

It was blocked with sticks and trees
But she paid no attention.
She hurried by just like a breeze
Until she felt a tension.

She didn't see him right away
But he tossed pinecones to her.
She threw them back day after day
Till learning something newer.

By snapping twigs and whistling
He taught her how to spot him
Through a low and leafy opening,
All colorful with autumn.

"You're super shy!" she laughed,
And Fever laughed right back.
"You sound just like me, copy-cat!
I'll bring you out a snack."

Next morning, Maggie skipped along
With apples in a basket.
Behind her snuck a worried man,
But this, she didn't know yet.

Arriving at their special place
She whistled for her friend.
But today was quite a different case—
Their fun was at an end.

Instead of Fever peeking out
A giant tree stump stood.
Two arms, two legs, a roaring mouth—
The ruler of the woods!

Maggie fainted toward the earth
But her daddy caught her.
Fever's daddy watched them both
Thinking, *Father...daughter.*

From behind a boulder
Sprang the boy, all cold with fear.
Climbing to those massive shoulders
He whispered in that great big ear.

Maggie woke up in her house
Parents pulling down the shades.
They certainly believed her now
But she'd gladly make a trade.

"If I can have my best friend back,"
She prayed up to the heavens,
"I promise to get back on track
And respect the woods they live in."

What a lonely time, that winter
For Fever and for Maggie.
His dreams were filled with folks like her.
Hers were filled with shaggy.

When springtime finally came around
The forest free of snow
On her windowsill she found
Seven crystals in a row!

The fun began again but changed.
They couldn't see each other.
Girl and boy could play their game
But it was called Discover.

Her parents were okay with this
And so was Fever's family—
Everybody in their place
Just where and when they should be.

One night, beneath a cloudy sky
A magic scene occurred.
The forest people blinked their eyes
And gazed without a word.

The moon emerged and showed the clan
Not close enough for harm.
Three tall ones stood, including Mom
With a baby in her arms.

Before the moonlight fell away
Maggie looked at Fever.
So much to wish, so much to say
But she knew he had to leave her.

They kept in touch across the years
By gifting at their spot

Till both were grown and nowhere near
But never far at heart.

Christopher Noël lives in northern Vermont, where he has often interacted with real Sasquatch people.

To see his videos and books go to:
www.TheNearnessofYou.net

Please go to hangar1publishing.com to stay up to date with the his newest releases.